LAOS
A Journey Beyond The Mekong

TEXT AND PHOTOGRAPHS BY
BEN DAVIES

ASIA HORIZONS BOOKS

Acknowledgements

Amongst the many people who helped me with this book, special thanks should go to Sayasouk of Sodetour and to the company's many excellent guides without whom I would not have had the opportunity to go so far off the beaten track. Dr. Chanthaphilith Chiemsisouraj, director general of the Ministry of Information and Culture and Bridget Page made valuable contributions as did Heather Peters at UNESCO, David Feingold of Ophidian Research Institute and Anna Källén, archaeologist at Lao Pako. To my wife Cristina, who encouraged me to do the project in the first place, thank you for your enthusiasm and understanding. A huge vote of thanks to friends and photographers Nic Dunlop, Adam Oswell, Olie Pin-Fat, Patrick Brown and Philip Blenkinsop for their advice and magnificent support and to Roland Neveu for his artistic inspiration and uncompromising photo editing. Finally, I would like to express my gratitude to Peter Neville who made this book possible.

Photography & text: Ben Davies
Picture editor: Roland Neveu
Editor: Graeme Loveridge
Cover design: Helen Kudrich
Publishing consultant: Peter Neville

First published by Luna Publications Ltd: April 2001
Second Edition: November 2007
Design and layout: Asia Horizons Books, Co. Ltd – info@asiahorizons.com

This project received generous support from NTEC, Ericsson and Sodetour.

This new edition (2007) is published by Asia Horizons Books Co., Ltd. – www.asiahorizons.com

ISBN: 978-974-09-1786-1

Lao Ministry of Information and Culture original registration: IE-AT 03/DEB 17102000 T 3000

MAP OF LAOS

YUNNAN

CHINA

BURMA

Jinghong

Phongsali • **Hat Sa**

VIETNAM

Ban Boun Tai

Muang Sing • **Boten**

Muang Khua

HANOI

MEKONG

Xieng Kok •

Ma

Luang Nam Tha

Pha

Muang Ngoi

Xieng Kho

Chiang Khong

BOKEO

Oudomxai **Pakmong**

Sam Neua • **Vieng Xai**

Houayxai

Pha Ou

Bak Ou

Pakbeng •

MEKONG

Pak Ou

Xuang

GULF OF TONKIN

⊙ **LUANG PRABANG**

Khan

XIENG KHUANG

Muang Kham

Sayaboury •

Kasi •

PLAIN OF JARS

Phonsavan

Phu Bia (2819)

Vinh

Van Vieng •

Ngum

BOLIKAMSAY

Pak Lai •

⊙ **Thalat**

Paksane

Kading

Laksao • *Cau Treo*

MEKONG

Ngum

⊙ **VIENTIANE**

Nong Khai

Hang Tao

Hin Boun

KHAMMUAN

Udon Thani

Nakhon Phanom

Tha Kaek

Sakhon Nakhon

THAILAND

Dong Ha

Sepon

Lao Bao

Mukdahan

Savannakhet

Muang Phin

HUÉ

Banghiang

Heuan Hin

Sekong

Atouat (2500)

Salavan

Sekong

Ubon Ratchathani

Vang Tao

Sedon

Tadlo

Paksong

Chongmek

Pakse

Attapeu

Champassak

WAT PHU

Qum Muang

Sekong

CAMBODIA

Don Khong

Ventkame

Lumphat

N
W E
S

0   50   100 km

LAOS
A JOURNEY BEYOND THE MEKONG

TEXT AND PHOTOGRAPHS BY
BEN DAVIES

FOREWORD

One summer's day in 1989, I caught a boat across the Mekong from the Thai border town of Nong Khai to Tha Deua in Laos. It was shortly after the communist country had begun to open its doors to the outside world and the place had a rare and surreal feel about it. In Vientiane, the sleepy Lao capital city, grass was growing up along the side streets. Many of the buildings remained in a state of graceful, but almost total decay.

Over the past fifteen years, as the country has gradually opened up, I have returned numerous times to Laos, travelling by road, by river and by elephant. Initially it was to Luang Prabang and Vientiane that I went. Then later to the forests and remote border provinces in the far north and south of the country.

Following roads and rivers to nowhere, I entered a world where despite recent progress, the rhythms of life are still largely tied to the soil, to the mountain spirits and to the chanting of Buddhist monks. My journey finished where it had started on the banks of the Mekong River, as it flowed down over the Khone Falls into the hazy distance, mixing memories of war with hopes for peace and prosperity.

ASIA'S FINAL FRONTIER

High up in the Annamite Mountains, a narrow road cuts through the remote northern province of Phongsali, weaving its way past a succession of rocky outcrops clothed in dense tropical vegetation. The landscape, as far as the eye can see, is made up of forest and spectacular limestone cliffs that rise up like jagged teeth above the ridges. A handful of minority villages cling to the dusty red slopes of the mountainside, their plumes of smoke tapering off into the distance. Nothing else moves on this wild and glorious terrain.

Descending into the sprawling town of Oudomxai, the route continues south towards Ban Pak Mong, a settlement situated on the banks of the Nam Bak River. Soon the grand and lofty mountain scenery gives way to rolling foothills and further off to the fertile plains irrigated by the waters of the Mekong - lifeline to this land-locked country. With a surface area of 235,000 square kilometers, slightly larger than Great Britain, Laos is one of Southeast Asia's final frontiers. Its landmass is predominantly mountainous, comprising rugged peaks and plateaus that slope down over the borders into neighbouring China, Vietnam, Burma, Cambodia and Thailand. Its people are ethnically diverse, ranging from the colourfully dressed Iko of the North to the remote and enigmatic Alak and Ta-oy tribes of the South.

The contrasts with neighbouring Thailand are especially striking. Whilst Thailand has modern highways, luxury hotels and giant factories spewing out almost every conceivable type of consumer good, Laos is poor and under-developed. Its five million inhabitants make this one of the least heavily populated countries in Asia. Its roads are few and far between. But like some rich and intricate tapestry, Laos contains a wealth of cultural, religious and scenic attractions, until recently closed off from the outside world. In Luang Prabang, the former royal capital, glittering pagodas line the banks of the Mekong and Nam Khan Rivers, sudden clusters of gold set amidst swaying palms. Further south in Champassak Province, the great mountain sanctuary of Wat Phu provides a stark reminder of the times when primitive gods were believed to hold sway over this proud and ancient land.

From the Lao capital Vientiane, on the banks of the Mekong, our eastward journey takes us through emerald green rice paddies bathed in the serene glow of the early-morning sun. Following roads and dirt tracks that criss-cross these immense tracts of land, we travel on to Phonsavan, home to the Plain of Jars and beyond to the remote provinces of Khammuan and Attapeu. It is here amidst the wild and rugged splendour of the landscape and the simple generosity of the people that the real spirit of Laos is to be found; a quiet yet elemental power that will always make this for me one of the most awesome countries in the region.

Ancient Kingdom

"Among the many powerful kingdoms of the farthest East of which we have scarcely heard of in Europe, there is one whose name is Laos, more properly known as the Kingdom of a Million Elephants," wrote Father Giovanni Filippo de Marini, one of the first Italian missionaries to visit the country, in 1640. A thousand years before Father Giovanni wrote these now memorable words, Laos was most probably inhabited by small groups of hunters, gatherers, farmers and settlers who produced pottery, textiles and basic metallurgical implements.

Recent archaeological excavations undertaken at Lao Pako to the north of Vientiane have unearthed more than 270 kilograms of potsherds and 45 complete buried jars as well as iron artefacts and stone tools. Using radiocarbon analysis, the site has been dated to between AD 400 and 600. The excavations, carried out by a Lao-Swedish research team, prove beyond reasonable doubt that Laos was inhabited during early times. They also raise the intriguing possibility that a flourishing Iron Age culture may well have existed in this part of the country at the same time as in Central Vietnam, Cambodia and Northeast Thailand. Sometime between the 8th and 13th centuries, the migration of successive waves of Tai people from Southern China signalled the emergence of a new order. Gradually the Tai displaced the existing Mon and Khmer people who lived along the fertile river valleys. It was only in 1353, however, that the first unified Lao kingdom was established under the legendary Prince Fa Ngum. It was named Lan Xang - The Kingdom of a Million Elephants.

Great Explorers

One of the first Europeans to travel into the heart of Laos was a French naturalist by the name of Henri Mouhot. After setting sail from London on a ship of 'very modest pretension', this remarkable Frenchman landed in Bangkok in September 1858, whereupon he received an audience with King Somdej Phra. He went on to visit Cambodia and the lost ruins of Angkor, before travelling by oxcart and elephant through the malaria-ridden jungles and bandit-infested plains of Siam and Laos to the royal city of Luang Prabang. Even in those days, the local people had a clearly identifiable character. "The Lhao appear to me to be more industrious than the Siamese, and above all, possess a much more adventurous and mercantile spirit," Mouhot wrote in his journals, which was published following his sudden death in November 1861.

Mouhot was particularly struck by the gracious and fun-loving nature of the Lao as well as by their gentle and tolerant nature. "The women are generally better looking than the Siamese," he observed. "They wear a single short petticoat of cotton, and sometimes a piece of silk over the breast." Other writers were equally captivated by the charm of the Lao as well as the magnificence of their country, covered in lush tropical vegetation and golden temples. "Oh what a delightful paradise," wrote Marthe Bassenne, a

French woman who travelled to Luang Prabang in 1909 and described her adventures in the book "In Laos and Siam."

It was in the late 19th century that Laos became a French protectorate. In one particularly brazen episode of gunboat diplomacy that occurred about this time, the French navy blockaded the entrance to the Chao Phaya River in 1893 and demanded that the King of Siam hand over parts of Cambodia and Laos to them. The French eventually won the day. But whilst Laos was to remain under French control for the next 50 years, it never provided its colonial masters with the riches that they had dreamed of.

There was, however, plenty of consolation. Despite their failure to achieve any notable material progress in Laos, the French administrators embraced the local culture with considerable enthusiasm. By the time that the well-known author Norman Lewis arrived in Vientiane in the early 1950s, many of the civil servants had taken on Lao wives, embraced Buddhism and adopted an 'untroubled and mildly libidinous' way of life.

Secret War

In the town of Muang Khun in Xieng Khuang Province, a giant statue of the Buddha stares serenely out over the surrounding hills. The 16th century statue has long been revered by the local people. But like the temple that once housed it, the Buddha is riddled with bomb shrapnel and bullets.

Throughout the remote central province of Xieng Khuang and to the east along the mountainous border with Vietnam, bomb craters the size of houses provide an ever present reminder of the bloody war that decimated vast areas of the country. Between 1964 and 1973, the US dropped more than 2 million tons of bombs on neutral Laos in a bid to defeat the communist-inspired Pathet Lao forces and destroy the North Vietnamese supply lines along the Ho Chi Minh Trail. The bombing campaign was probably the largest ever mounted in modern history and left as many as 50,000 dead.

Almost as damaging as the raids carried out by the lumbering B-52 aircraft was the use of defoliants and herbicides. Chemical weapons such as Agent Orange poisoned the water and irrigation systems and destroyed the vegetation. Tens of thousands of innocent civilians suffered from the effects of 'yellow rain' as well as from cluster bombs specially designed to inflict maximum damage on the local population. Yet until October 1969, this war was kept secret from the American people – the result of a high level cover-up by the US government supported by a clandestine force made up of CIA officers, Green Berets and US trained mercenaries.

American involvement in Laos, however, was to end in failure just as it had in neighbouring Vietnam and Cambodia. On 23 August 1975, only months after the fall of Phnom Penh and Saigon, the victorious Pathet Lao seized the capital Vientiane and shortly afterwards announced the foundation of the Lao People's Democratic Republic.

Mother River

It's a two-day journey south from the bombed-out tableland known as the Plain of Jars to the Mekong River, lifeline to the tumultuous region of Indochina. From its source high up on the icy Tibetan Plateau, 'the Mother River' tumbles down through the mountain gorges of Southwestern China, passing through the fertile plains of Burma and Thailand before entering Laos near the town of Huay Xai. Traversing the infamous Golden Triangle, the river then cuts east past the ancient city of Luang Prabang, cradle of Lao civilization, before rejoining the border with Thailand.

Nobody who has travelled along this magnificent stretch of water can fail to be impressed by its varied landscape, its sudden and unexpected rapids, nor by the legends that surround the river. One giant species of catfish that inhabit the Mekong measures 2-3 metres long and weighs up to 300 kg, making it the largest freshwater fish in the world. Superstitious locals believe that the Pla Buk, more widely known as the Monster of the Mekong, is the reincarnation of fishermen who drowned in the river.

In June 1866, a French expedition set sail from the Cochin Chinese port of Saigon in a bid to become the first country to navigate the full length of the river. The gunboats, under the command of Captain Doudart de Lagree and Francis Garnier, eventually reached Luang Prabang and the upper reaches of the Mekong. But French dreams of establishing a major trade route between China and Vietnam were shattered by a succession of rapids and repeated attacks by bandits. More than a century later, the Mekong is once again being touted as a catalyst for regional economic development. Two giant hydro-electricity dams have already been constructed in central and eastern Laos. As many as 20 other dams are undergoing feasibility and environmental studies. If completed, the government claims that the dams could one day bring new prosperity to the people of this impoverished nation.

Beyond the Pha Peng Falls in the southern-most province of Champassak, the Mekong crosses over the border into Cambodia and Vietnam before eventually splitting into the nine channels known as the 'Nine Dragons,' or Cuu Long, and emptying out into the South China Sea.

Way of Life

At dusk, the sound of monks chanting fills the inner sanctuary of Wat Si Sakhet in Vientiane, their voices echoing through the confines of this revered temple. To celebrate Visakha Puja, one of the holiest occasions in the Buddhist calendar, the faithful come from all over the city to light candles and incense sticks and to parade three times around the temple courtyard. The procession, which is held in May, recalls the birth, enlightenment and death of the Buddha.

In the lowland regions of Laos, almost every boy and girl has heard the story of Siddharta Gautama, the young prince who gave up the promise of enormous wealth, a glittering palace and a wife and children in order to search for the ultimate truths. Seeking to rid himself of all worldly desires, the future Buddha battled with the temptress Mara, overcoming storms, sudden floods and famine in his quest for spiritual peace. Exhausted, he meditated for seven days and seven nights under a Bodhi tree before achieving a state of enlightenment and universal knowledge.

Introduced to Laos during the late 13th or early 14th centuries, Buddhism teaches that suffering is an inevitable part of desire and that only by extinguishing desire can the mind and body be at peace. Many young men will spend a part of their lives in the temple as a monk or novice, learning the scriptures and accumulating merit for themselves and for their families in the hope that they will be reborn into a better life. Women cannot become monks, but they can improve their karma by performing good deeds and following the humble example of the Buddha.

Baci Ceremony

One April afternoon, an old man invites me into his house to share in a simple act of friendship and good will. We are in the village of Ban Phonmuang, a short distance from Savannakhet. Inside his wooden house are several village elders as well as family members and their friends. They sit cross-legged around a low table on which rests a basket filled with fruits and money, donated by many of the guests.

Known as the Baci, this ceremony is the single most important animist ritual in all of Laos and reflects the traditional belief that the human body is made up of 32 spirits, or khouan. To make sure that these spirits do not wander too far afield, offerings of food, incense and flowers are made to appease the khouan and to restore the body's harmony. Even amongst Buddhist faithful, who account for some 60% of the Lao population, the Baci is a widely accepted practice.

Taking my wrist in her hand, an old woman mumbles a few words of blessing in a mixture of the Pali and Lao languages, calling on the spirits to bring me good fortune, peace and health. May he have many water buffalo, many children, much fruit and a large

crop of rice, she says. Afterwards a half-dozen simple white cotton threads, or saisins, are tied around my wrist by the old woman and by several other relatives and friends of the family. The Lao believe that so long as the baci-cords remain around the wrist, they will bring good luck. Sometimes the Baci ceremony will be held to celebrate a wedding; on other occasions to celebrate the arrival of a newborn baby or any other auspicious event. Almost everywhere in Laos, however, it is viewed as the most effective means of winning the favour of the spirits whose support is deemed vital for any human endeavour.

Ethnic Minorities

Beyond the banks of the Mekong River, the sweeping valleys and rice fields of the lowlands give way to the hills of the North, home to one of the most diverse ethnic populations in Southeast Asia. Officially the country has 68 different ethnic groups together with a host of relatively unknown tribes and jungle nomads. Some minorities like the Hmong people live high up on the steep mountain slopes growing dried rice and vegetables or harvesting opium. Others like the Alak, the Ta-oy and the Khatu prefer to live at lower levels in the southern part of the country where they survive mainly on subsistence farming and animal husbandry.

Ethnologists typically classify the Lao people into three distinctive groups. The most numerous are the Lao Loum or lowland people. Comprising an estimated 60% of the population, they generally inhabit the rich farmlands and floodlands along the Mekong where they cultivate rice, practice Theravada Buddhism and wield much of the country's political and economic power. Renown for their charm and affability, the Lao Loum are above all famous for their unhurried pace of life, summed up in the much repeated phrase "Baw pen nyang" meaning "no problems."

The second largest group in the country is commonly known as the Lao Theung. Making up about a quarter of the population, this Sino-Tibetan people occupy the lower mountain slopes, especially in the northern region and on the Bolovens Plateau to the south, practising slash and burn farming and growing coffee, glutinous rice and tobacco. The third group, classified as the Lao Soung, live at higher elevations than the other minorities. These hilltribes, whose numbers include the Iko and the Yao, settled in Laos long after the arrival of the other groups. As a result, they were forced to occupy the most inhospitable mountainous regions in the far north of the country and around Xieng Khouang Province.

In recent times, however, the rigid classification of the ethnic minorities has become increasingly less relevant as lowlanders have moved up into the hills in search of new land to farm, displacing many of the highland people. Even in the fertile plains and along the banks of the Mekong, large-scale migration is leading to a blurring of ethnic lines.

Changing Seasons

It is in the months from November to January that the Lao countryside is at its most beautiful, the villages shrouded in a veil of early morning mist that dissipates slowly over the surrounding hills. This is the time of year when the poor farming communities of the lowlands are at their busiest and when entire families descend on the paddies to harvest the fields of ripened rice. From February to March, the mountains of the North are covered with yellow and white blossoms as wild flowers and opium poppies bloom on the hillside. As temperatures rise, the once tumultuous streams and waterfalls are reduced to a trickle. Soon the landscape becomes harsh and arid, the earth scorched by the midday sun.

April and May are the hottest months of the year when the farmers burn off their fields and plough the soil in preparation for the rains to come. By the end of June, the hazy skies have given way to storm clouds. The monsoons bring sudden respite to the rural people and life to the parched landscape. For several months, many roads become impassable, except by four-wheel drive or elephant. Rivers burst their banks and countless villages are cut off from the major towns. Only in October, do the rains come to an end and the local people take to the fields once again, signalling the beginning of a new cycle.

Colourful Ceremonies

My return to Luang Prabang coincides with one of the greatest festivals in the Lao calendar. It is April and the temples are filled with people sprinkling holy water over Buddha images to celebrate the New Year known as "pi mai". Out on the streets passers-by throw buckets of water at each other in a symbolic show of spiritual cleansing. In one of the great highlights of the festival, a procession of elephants, beauty queens and colourful floats parades through the town accompanied by the legendary figures of Pou Nyer and Nyar Nyer – two of the most famous ancestors of the Lao people – dressed in dazzling red masks.

The New Year Festival is only one of a host of celebrations held throughout the country. In May, the people signal the end of the dry season by firing giant homemade rockets up into the clouds to remind the god of rain that it is time for the start of the annual monsoons. Traditionally the villagers believed that when the god heard the sound of frogs croaking from below, he would realize that there was sufficient rain and would halt the monsoons until the following year.

Further south in the fertile plains, I stumble across a succession of other festivals: colourful boat races, thanks-giving ceremonies, weddings and sometimes even funerals – all conducted with the same wholesome spontaneity and joie de vivre that is a hallmark of this vibrant country.

Opening page: Annamite Mountain Range, Xieng Khuang Province.

Left: Limestone cliffs, Vieng Xai District, Hua Phan Province.

Following pages:
Left: Slowboats on the Mekong, Luang Prabang.
Right: Monsoon clouds over the Mekong, Pakbeng, Bokeo Province.

Elephant camp in the jungle, Sayaboury Province.

Top: Village life, Ban Dong Dan, Phonsavanh District.
Bottom: Workers descend the mountainside before dawn, Sayaboury Province.

Poppy fields at harvest-time, Phongsali Province.

Dirt tracks through remote Attapeu Province.

Left page, top: Stone Forest at dusk, Khammuan Province.
Bottom: Taat Fan Waterfall, Paksong, Champassak Province.
Right page: River bank, Vang Vieng.

TRIBES IN THE MIST

North of Luang Nam Tha, the mountains rise up into an unbroken chain extending over the border into neighbouring China and Vietnam. The terrain is rugged with few roads. Most villages are situated at great distances from one another, connected by a network of slippery paths that snake their way over the hillside like endless strips of ribbon. During the winter months, from November through to February, temperatures can fall to below zero, whilst during the monsoons the furthest flung settlements are virtually cut off by floods and landslides.

On this isolated and in many ways inhospitable landscape live the ethnic minorities collectively known as the hilltribes. Ranging from the Yao or the Mien to the Lahu, the Iko and the Hmong, they are amongst the poorest and the most diverse of the Lao peoples. History traces the origins of these hilltribes mainly to China and Tibet, from where over the centuries they spread into the Shan States of Burma, Vietnam and Northern Thailand. Nowadays they are mainly concentrated in the Northern Provinces of Laos as well as in the border territories, where they live in primitive settlements roughly hewn out of the mountainside.

It is late afternoon when we reach the village of Phouyair, situated high up in the hills, a three-day walk from Muang Sing. A simple gateway consisting of two pillars supporting a lintel is all that marks the entrance to the village. Below, a collection of huts on stilts falls away down the hillside, their interiors blackened by acrid smoke. In this remote settlement to the east of the Mekong, the villagers head out into the forests at dawn to forage for wood or for lizards, squirrel, snakes and deer which they kill with old-fashioned shotguns and eat to supplement their diet of rice and vegetables. A handful of women and children stay at home, pounding corn with giant pestles or collecting water from the stream below. Only the sick and infirm are absolved from this daily toil.

But the fragile existence of these shy mountain people is being threatened by the gradual opening up of the country and the rapid depletion of its natural resources. Whereas once they could rely on the surrounding jungles to provide them with food, timber and fertile soil, now they are reduced in many cases to subsistence farming. New schools and the advent of new roads are also fast transforming the world of the hilltribes, eroding the traditions that have been passed down over the years. And whilst progress is helping to integrate the people into the mainstream of Lao life, it is also leading to a loss of identity with many minority peoples turning to opium as an escape from an increasingly harsh existence.

Mountain Spirits

The people of the Yao tribe have a superstition. They believe that if a villager falls sick, it is because the soul has left the human body. As soon as this misfortune occurs, a shaman or spirit doctor will be called upon to make propitious offerings of a slaughtered pig or paper money to the ancestors who will help to lure back the wandering spirit. Only when the soul has returned to its rightful place in the body will the patient recover and the ritual offerings come to an end.

Animism continues to influence the daily lives of almost all the minority people in one way or another. Some hilltribes hold an annual ceremony to honour the spirit of Crop Grandmother who has the power to bring good and bad harvests. Others place offerings of food, rice whisky and joss sticks inside miniature shrines to give thanks to the Lord of Land and Water. Rice spirits are treated with special respect. Before planting can begin, the Iko must be sure to locate a site where the spirit of the rice will feel comfortable for the duration of the season. If a wild pig or a barking deer is seen running away from the chosen site, the plot will immediately be abandoned and a new one found. Failure to act will almost inevitably lead to drought or some other natural disaster.

Magnificent Attire

At dawn we leave the village, climbing up into the mists past a scattering of opium fields and rows of neatly planted cabbages. Soon the shallow hillside gives way to dusty-red slopes and further off to the stilted houses of the Iko, clinging to the mountainside.

Anthropologists trace the origins of the colourfully dressed Iko to Yunnan Province in Southern China, from where they migrated along the Black and Red Rivers, first to Burma and then later to Vietnam, Laos and Thailand. Settling in the mountainous districts of Luang Nam Tha, Oudomxai and Phongsali Provinces, this remarkable people prefer to live above an elevation of 1,000 metres, where they grow dry rice, raise pigs and chickens and occasionally cultivate opium.

Like other minorities, the Iko take a fierce pride in their past. According to one ancient myth, the all-powerful god Apoe Miyeh created the first Iko man and woman as well as the earth and the sky. To ensure that the people would live together in harmony, Apoe Miyeh handed out instructions to the village representatives written on the skin of a water buffalo. Those instructions form 'the Iko Way', a philosophy that influences almost every aspect of the people's lives from worship of the spirits to cultivation of the rice fields. From an early age, the Iko are taught to recall the names of all their ancestors in the male line for up to 13 generations. Respect for the village elders and for the recently deceased members of the tribe are also viewed as vital to the peaceful co-existence of the people.

More than just their rich traditions and beliefs, the Iko are famous for their prodigious weaving skills and their magnificent outfits. Whilst the men sometimes wear loose trousers, an embroidered jacket and a flat turban, which resembles a beret, the women have short skirts, ankle putties and sashes often decorated with brightly coloured beads. Their crowning glory, however, is a headdress the size of a motorbike helmet, encrusted with silver spheres and coins and often dating back to the French colonial era. The houses of the Iko are also clearly distinguishable from those of other hilltribes. They are raised on wooden posts with sweeping roofs and an uncovered platform at the front. Inside, there are two main sections, one for the men and one for the women. There is also a simple altar containing offerings of food and drink for the ancestors who provide the Iko with a sense of continuity in their lives and a source of hope for the future.

Village Festivities

In the cool of December, two months after the annual monsoon rains have finished, the Hmong prepare to celebrate the start of their New Year. Out in the fields, the villagers rebuild fences and clear away shrubbery in readiness for the next planting season. Most women and children stay at home to ferment rice wine in giant vats or to round up pigs, chickens, cows and water buffalo to be sacrificed and eaten in the course of the festivities.

During the celebrations held in Hmong villages throughout the country, the people sing, dance, drink and play games that have been handed down from generation to generation. In one of the most popular games, the boys and girls, dressed in finely embroidered jackets with pink and red pom poms, line up opposite one another and play catch with a ball made from black cloth. First a girl will throw the ball to the boy that she likes best. Then the boys will reciprocate. These childish pursuits, however, are not entirely innocent. By the end of the festivities that last anything up to two weeks, many of the boys and girls will have paired off as a prelude to marriage.

The Hmong are not the only hilltribe to celebrate the New Year with such a surfeit of enthusiasm. The Iko, the Phou Noi and the Thai Deng also hold similar festivities at other times of the year.

Not to be outdone, the Yao people even celebrate a funeral with three days and three nights of continuous drinking and feasting.

Papaver Somniferum

In late January and early February, some areas of the mountainous North and Northeast are dotted with the brightly coloured red and white poppies known as Papaver Somniferum. These flowers are amongst the most beautiful and innocuous looking in Southeast Asia and have been used by the hill tribes in China for medicinal purposes for hundreds of years. But the poppies also produce opium resin – the key ingredient for heroin, one of the world's most dangerous drugs.

Cultivated on the higher mountain slopes where the soil and temperatures are more supportive, the poppies are planted at the end of the wet season in late September or early October. When they are ready for harvesting three months later, the hilltribes cut neat vertical incisions into the pods, allowing the resin to leak out and congeal in the sun. The resulting gum is then scraped off, rolled into balls and wrapped in dried poppy petals or banana leaves before being sold in raw form to foreign middlemen.

Grown in Asia since the 13th century, at the time of Kublai Khan, opium production in the region increased dramatically during the 1960s and early 1970s when the US encouraged its cultivation in order to finance their clandestine war in parts of Indochina. These days consumption amongst the ethnic minorities is once again rising as the people find themselves alienated from their old way of life. At night in some hilltribe villages, the sweet sickly smell of opium drifts through the bamboo rafters. The addicts, their faces lit by flickering candles, lie on the floor smoking up to 20 pipes a day as they float off into their own private world.

Traditionally it is believed that opium makes the people strong. Yet many addicts are unable to work or to look after their children. The government, supported by the UN and drug enforcement agencies, is now attempting to eradicate opium production by encouraging alternative cash crops such as rice, coffee, beans and garlic. But their efforts are stymied by the remoteness of the poppy fields, together with the high price that opium commands in world markets.

Fierce Independence

The narrow trail twists up into the hills above Muang Ngoi, winding its way past clumps of bamboo and blackened tree trunks. Beyond the ridge we catch our first glimpse of the Hmong village; a cluster of huts set in the shape of a horseshoe around a dusty yard. If the Iko believe in the all-powerful Apoe Miyeh, the Hmong claim that the earth was created thousands of years ago by the spirit of the sky. With their heavy silver jewellery, their pleated skirts and their black leggings, this proud and warrior-like people are the most independent of the hilltribes. Tracing their origins back to China – and possibly even to Tibet, Siberia and Mongolia – the Hmong prefer to live high up in the mountains. During the Vietnam war, they sided against the communists. Many fled over the border into Thailand following the end of the war. Others remained in the hills where sporadic resistance continues to this day.

Widely acknowledged as the hardest working of the hilltribes, the Hmong are well known for their riding prowess and their love of alchohol. When the writer Norman Lewis came across them in the 1950s, he marvelled at their extravagant embroidery and their enormous turbans. Other foreigners were more excited by the existence of love groves where the young unmarried Hmong women would freely bestow their favours on willing young men. When French civil servants took up their posts in the late 19th and early 20th century, they are believed to have invested considerable amounts of time and money securing maps with the precise locations of these groves.

Opening page: Iko ceremonial swing, Ban Long Muay, Luang Nam Tha Province.
Above: Katu settlement, Ban Kop Phum, Bolovens Plateau.

Opium addict, Phongsali Province, Northern Laos.

Early morning mist rises above the Iko village of Sopee. This poor settlement is situated high up in the hills, a three day walk from Muang Sing in the northern province of Luang Nam Tha.

Top: Yao child at Ban Pa, near the border with Vietnam, Hua Phan Province.
Bottom: Portrait of a village elder, Hua Phan Province.
Right page: Transporting the harvest, Ban Bien, Vieng Thong District.

Minority villagers trudging through the monsoon-drenched countryside.

Talat Nyai, one of the most popular markets for the minority peoples of the North, Muang Sing.

Mountain transport along the rugged border territory, Muang Ngoen District, Sayaboury Province.

Top: Village scene, Ban Hao Huay, Phongsali Province.
Bottom: A newly married Iko woman departs for the seven hour walk to the nearest town.
Following pages, left: The Nam Ou, Muang Khua. Right: Ban Songcha, Oudomxai Province.

Above: Woman fetching water in the remote village of Phouyair, Luang Nam Tha Province.

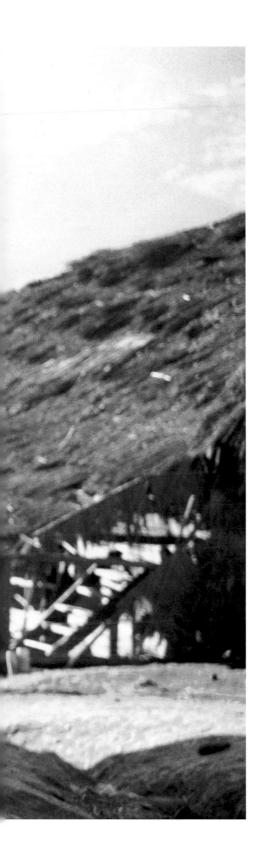

Top: Iko portrait up in the hills of Oudomxai Province.
Bottom: Ban Paknam Noi on market day, Phongsali Province.

LAND OF A MILLION ELEPHANTS

There can be few more enchanting places on earth than Luang Prabang, sitting at the confluence of the Mekong and Nam Khan Rivers, surrounded by flame trees and a profusion of tropical palms. As the Mekong curves east around the entrance to the Pak Ou Caves, the limestone cliffs give way to gentler hills. Canoes dart across the surface of the water powered by noisy longtail engines or occasionally propelled by oars. A few small fishing villages cling to the banks of the river. Finally we round the last corner to catch a glimpse of the golden spires of Luang Prabang.

According to an ancient legend, two hermit brothers, who were combing the northern foothills for a spiritual retreat, stumbled across this site more than a thousand years ago. The brothers predicted that this peaceful valley, surrounded on three sides by water, would one day become a powerful kingdom ruled over by a succession of monarchs. There is, however, another story that is also widely believed. Some locals claim that it was the Buddha himself who first came across this tranquil spot and as proof of his discovery left a three metre footprint near a rocky outcrop at Wat Siphuthabaht.

Situated a day's drive from the modern Lao capital Vientiane, Luang Prabang's temples, its gilded reliefs and cool promenades provide travellers with the ultimate retreat from the pressures of the modern world. In the shadow of perfumed forests, you can literally soothe your senses, lulled by the tinkling of bells and the chanting of monks.

To see Luang Prabang at its most magical, get up at dawn and wander down the narrow backstreets, where lines of monks on their daily alms round receive offerings of rice and fruit from the Buddhist faithful. Momentarily, the town is filled with languid figures clad in saffron robes. Then almost as suddenly as they have appeared, they stride off into the distance, returning to their Buddhist retreats in leafy compounds dotted around the city. Elsewhere on this sleepy peninsula, home to the Royal Palace and the revered Prabang Buddha image, history mingles with religion, providing a reminder of the days when this region was known as Lan Xang, Land of a Million Elephants and the White Parasol.

Royal City

Historians trace the origins of the city of Luang Prabang to some time between the 6th and 8th centuries when it formed part of an early Mon principality named Muang Sua. For almost 500 years, it remained lost in the mists of time until the legendary conqueror King Fa Ngum rebelled against his grandfather and established the city as the capital of a loose collection of states. Although scholars dispute the full extent of its power, Lan Xang in its heyday is believed to have held sway over much of Cambodia as well as parts of China, the Korat Plateau in Northeast Thailand and the Annamite Mountains. To the south, its borders extended far beyond the present-day capital Vientiane

Under a succession of kings, the greatest being King Setthathirat, Buddhism was adopted as the state religion, spawning a host of opulent temples. In 1513, Wat Visoun was constructed in honour of the revered Prabang statue, after which the city was named. Reputed to have originally come from Ceylon (Sri Lanka) in the 3rd century, this priceless statue made from gold, silver and bronze is widely believed to have magical powers. Several rare Buddha images, including a giant bronze cast measuring six metres high and weighing two tons, were placed in Luang Prabang's other temples. By the middle of the 18th century, the city played host to some 65 temples spread out along the riverbanks.

Against all the odds, many of these temples survived despite repeated incursions by the Burmese, the Siamese, the Khmer and even the marauding Ho of China. In 1887, the Chinese from Yunnan attacked the city and destroyed some of its finest monuments. Yet Luang Prabang was to experience a renaissance in the following years, providing a home to the French vice-consul and to the Lao royal family. It remained a royal centre until the take-over by the Pathet Lao in 1975.

"Were it not for the constant blaze of a tropical sun, or if the mid-day heat were tempered by a gentle breeze, the place would be a little paradise," wrote the Frenchman Henri Mouhot on arriving in Luang Prabang in 1861. Mouhot, who is credited with rediscovering Angkor Wat in neighbouring Cambodia, never returned to his homeland. He died several months after setting foot in Laos following a sudden bout of malaria. His simple grave can be seen a short distance from Luang Prabang near the village of Ban Phanom, a whitewashed tomb sheltered by a scattering of trees and bushes.

Forgotten Corner

Countless other foreigners were also captivated by this northern city. In 1883, Herbert Warrington Smyth, a British national working for the Siamese government, lovingly described the red-tiled roofs of Luang Prabang's temples glimpsed amongst the coconut groves and dominated by a large hill in the centre of town.

Long before Mouhot and Warrington Smyth found their way to this remote corner of the earth, the Dutch had already discovered Luang Prabang. Gerrit van Wuystoff, a well-known merchant, reputedly came here in 1641. Some Jesuit missionaries may have crossed into Northern Laos at an even earlier date in a bid to convert the natives to christianity.

One of the most memorable descriptions of Luang Prabang came from the American writer Harry Franck. "Luang Prabang town is in many ways what idealists picture the cities of Utopia to be," he wrote in his book "East of Siam", which was published in the late 1920s. "It is not a city at all in the western sense, but a leisurely congregation of dwellings of simple lines." In recognition of the city's unique cultural and historical significance, UNESCO designated Luang Prabang a World Heritage Site in 1995. The decision is likely to ensure that the city can be admired by future generations.

Exquisite Architecture

The most striking of all Luang Prabang's temples lies a short distance to the north of town near the peninsula formed by the Mekong and Nam Khan. Wat Xieng Tong, known as the Golden City Monastery, is widely recognized as the finest example of Luang Prabang's architectural style. Influenced by the classical arts of neighbouring India, Ceylon and Cambodia as well as the works of the Dvarati, Mon and Lanna periods, its exquisite façade, its splendid mosaics and graceful sloping roofs bear witness to the unparalleled level of craftsmanship achieved during this era.

When the people of Luang Prabang first decided to build a temple here, they came across a Thong tree the colour of red lacquer. To commemorate the tree and the brightly coloured flowers that surrounded it, they created an elegant mosaic on the rear wall of the ordination hall using red glass inlay. A profusion of bougainvillea and bamboo fills the adjacent compound, lending this royal temple an air of quiet and dignified beauty.

From Wat Xieng Thong, it's a pleasant stroll down the main street past giant golden Buddhas and lavishly decorated temple facades to Wat Mai Suwannaphumaham, another of Luang Prabang's architectural feats. A former home of the Buddhist leader Phra Sangkharath, this remarkable building is decorated with bas-reliefs of pure gold depicting one of the last reincarnations of the Buddha. Inaugurated in 1788, its crowning attraction is a five-tiered roof, which reportedly took more than 70 years to complete.

In the late afternoon, as the sun begins its descent over the mountains to the west, the finest place to be in Luang Prabang is on the summit of Mount Phousi, literally translated as 'marvellous mountain'. From this lofty summit, next to the shimmering golden spire of Wat Chom Si, the town can be seen in all its glory, surrounded by forests and hills with small temple courtyards glimpsed far below like the sections of a doll's house.

Boat Racing

In September, as the northern monsoon rains give way to the first clear days of spring, the people of Luang Prabang come together to celebrate one of their most important festivals. To mark the end of the three-month Buddhist Lenten retreat, dozens of finely-carved long boats are carried down to the banks of the Nam Khan in preparation for the annual boat racing. Before engaging in the races, the teams visit the nearby temples to make offerings to the Buddha and to ask the various spirits for strength and good fortune. Afterwards, as cheering groups of supporters gather on both banks of the river, the sleek boats covered in garlands of sweet smelling flowers, race each other for up to a thousand metres, propelled by formidable teams of rowers brandishing tiny wooden paddles.

For the winners of this fiercely contested knockout competition, there is the prospect of fame and glory throughout the surrounding towns and villages, whilst for the losers, there is an abundance of rice wine and whisky as well as the distant hope of victory the following year.

Luang Prabang is just one of several riverine towns to hold a boat racing festival. In Vientiane, in Champassak and even in Savannakhet, boat racing is held in the weeks following the end of the rainy season. Water plays an integral part in other festivals too. For Songkran, when people throughout the country welcome in the Lao New Year, the inhabitants of Luang Prabang take to the river in their thousands, criss-crossing the Mekong in a joyous convoy of over-laden boats. Along the far bank they build miniature temples made from sand and decorated with banners depicting mythical animals of the Lao Zodiac. Elsewhere they sprinkle water over the Buddha images and over each other in the greatest ritual celebration of this life-giving force.

Beyond Luang Prabang the temples disappear from view, swallowed up by the rugged northern landscape and by the broad reaches of the Mekong snaking its way through the remote countryside. It was here, almost 100 years ago, that a medical doctor, who accompanied the Franco-Siamese border delimitation mission along this stretch of the river, came to grief on the rapids. The tragedy happened when his raft, made of two pirogues tied together was engulfed by a whirlpool and sucked into the abyss.

River Voyage

In the cool of the morning the river is grey and foreboding. Occasionally, our boat passes villages where plumes of smoke rise into the air from primitive stoves and where the cries of children can be heard above the steady roar of the engine. Further upstream, the Nam Ou River branches off from the Mekong, leading through a wilderness of hills and gigantic limestone cliffs that tower overhead like cathedral spires shrouded in lush vegetation. Leaving the towns of Muang Ngoi and Muang Khua behind, we enter the northern-most province of Phongsali, wedged between the borders of China and Vietnam. Here, the faces of the people are different, the dialect more akin to the people of Southern China than to mainstream Lao. Many of the houses would not look out of place over the border in the province of Yunnan. Even the markets sell Chinese beer and textiles.

North of Ban Hatsa, the scenery is at its most dramatic. Beyond the village of Ban Botay, sprawling at the foot of the hillside, the Nam Ou twists around giant boulders and sudden gorges, dividing here and there into narrow channels, before disappearing over the horizon.

Opening page: A young novice strolls through the leafy grounds of Wat Aham, Luang Prabang.

Left: Dawn over the banks of the Khan River in Luang Prabang, viewed from the forested slopes of Mount Phousi.

Top: Monks at Wat Visoun, known as the Watermelon Stupa. – bottom: Wat Xieng Thong.
Right page: Rennovating a stupa, Wat Aham.

Tourists and miniature Buddha statues at the Pak Ou Caves, Luang Prabang.

15th and 16th century Buddha statues, Wat Visoun, Luang Prabang.

Monks on their early morning alms round, Luang Prabang.

Elephants and their mahouts in search of work, Muang Ngoi District.

Left: That Chomsi on the summit of Mount Phousi, Luang Prabang.
Above: The 16th century royal temple of Wat Xieng Thong.

Traditional Lao New Year celebrations, Luang Prabang.

A New Year's procession through the streets of Luang Prabang.

59

Preceding pages: New Year festivities on the banks of the Mekong.
Above: Family Baci ceremony, Luang Prabang.

Offerings to the Buddha, Wat Mai Suwannaphumaham, Luang Prabang.

Boat racing festival on the Nam Khan River, Luang Prabang.

64

Top and bottom: Boat racing festival, Luang Prabang.

Monks join in the fun during the three day Songkran festival, Luang Prabang.

Transporting the venerated Pha Bang statue from the Royal Palace to Wat Mai.

Monsoon season in the northern hills of Luang Prabang Province.

Top: Vieng Thong District at dawn, Hua Phan Province.
Bottom: Boatmen on the Mekong, Luang Prabang.

LAO LOUM COUNTRY

The Lao Loum have a legend. They believe that the first Lao people were produced many thousands of years ago during the rule of the great terrestrial prince Pu Lan Xong. According to this popular story, which has been passed down from generation to generation, the ruler of the heavens ordered Pu Lan Xong to pierce a giant gourd, which had suddenly appeared out of the earth's surface. Following his orders, Pu Lan Xong took out his lance and punctured the large fleshy fruit. As if by magic, the first fair-skinned Lao Thai marched out. But the gourd continued to grow, so Pu Lan Xong pierced it once again and this time a darker skinned race emerged.

The Lao Loum like to tell this story to explain their country's ethnic diversity and the sheer numbers of different tribes and minorities who co-exist throughout this mountainous region. There are plenty of other myths and legends that are widely believed by the Lao Loum. Before taking a long journey or making an important decision in life, these superstitious people will typically hold a Baci ceremony to appease their guardian spirits. At planting or harvest time, they will make offerings to the spirits who inhabit the rice fields, whilst throughout their lives they will make certain that any significant celebration, such as a wedding, a funeral or a temple festival coincides with an auspicious date.

Known as lowlanders - because they generally live in the fertile valleys of the Mekong and along its rich network of streams and tributaries - the Lao Loum are the dominant ethnic group in the country, accounting for some sixty percent of the population. Predominately rice farmers, their largest concentrations are to be found in and around the cities of Vientiane, Luang Prabang, Savannakhet and Pakse, although increasingly they have settled in more mountainous regions.

Tall and gracious with high cheekbones and fairer skin, the features of the Lao Loum traditionally set them aside from the mountain people who are of Mon-Khmer descent. According to early reports by missionaries, the lowlanders also displayed a different temperament. The Lao Loum "are very docile and have a very good nature and are great friends with the tranquillity and the peace," wrote the Italian Jesuit Father de Marini in 1640. When Warrington Smyth travelled here two hundred years later, he went a step further, describing a people of great charm and conviviality with a love of native liquor and a particular relish for opium.

Walled City

The first Lao city that you reach if you travel north over the Lao Australian Friendship Bridge at Nong Khai, is the sleepy capital of Vientiane. Founded in 1560 by King Setthathirat, it went on to eclipse Luang Prabang. The name literally translates as "the walled city of the moon". Europeans who arrived in Vientiane in the 18th and early 19th centuries were much impressed by this prosperous town, shaded by palm trees and filled with splendid palaces, libraries and Buddhist monuments. John Crawford, the British emissary to Thailand claimed that the city was even more populous than Bangkok at the time.

Vientiane's days of glory, however, were numbered. In 1828, the Siamese army under general Mom Hao Thap razed the city, destroying almost every single temple except Wat Sisaket and force marching tens of thousands of Lao captives to Bangkok. For the next 50 years Vientiane was abandoned to the monsoon rains and the jungle. "Here, just like in Angkor, the tropical vegetation has thrown a veil over so many disasters," wrote one French woman in November 1909. "Unfortunately, the roots of the giant trees have continued the Siamese work of destruction."

In the late 19th century, the French began the laborious task of re-building the capital. To the original temples, which they cleared of undergrowth, the French added rambling colonial villas, grand administrative buildings and broad tree-lined boulevards – typical of the architectural style they used throughout Indochina. Into this melting-pot went colonaded shophouses, bakeries, a few breezy squares and even a Beaux-Arts-style presidential palace which they constructed adjacent to Wat Phra Kaeo, the former royal chapel. In the years since, Vientiane has received new architectural impetus with a Parisienne style Arc de Triomphe, as well as a handful of austere-looking government buildings. What remains today is a delightful if incongruous mix of styles that can be found in few other cities around the region.

Golden Spire

"A huge pyramid with a top covered in gold leaf weighing a thousand pounds," wrote the Dutch envoy Gerrit van Wuystoff, on visiting Vientiane's greatest Buddhist monument in 1641. Built almost one hundred years earlier in 1566, That Luang is widely viewed as the single most important religious monument in Laos, as well as an enduring symbol of Lao sovereignty. Reputed to contain a part of the Buddha's breastbone, it was believed to have been built on the site of an earlier temple constructed in the 3rd century AD by emissaries of the Mogul Emperor.

The history of That Luang in many ways mirrors the tumultuous history of this nation. During the 17th and 18th centuries, it was plundered by the warring Burmese and the Chinese Ho who raided Laos to exact revenge on its inhabitants and to capture some of the country's rare white elephants. In the early 19th century it was virtually destroyed by the Siamese. Finally, in 1893, it was struck by a bolt of lightning, which caused the spire to collapse. After being renovated by the French, That Luang's dazzling golden spire today dominates the northeast of the city, a symbol of eternity decorated with lotus petals and stylized banana flowers.

Besides That Luang, Vientiane boasts several other fine temples. To the west, between the morning market and the river, lies Wat Sisakhet, one of the city's few surviving monuments dating back to the 19th century. Built in 1818 by King Anouvong, this magnificent temple complex boasts more than 2,000 Buddha statues made from terracotta, bronze and wood and set in small niches around a central courtyard. Not to be outdone, the nearby Wat Ongtu (temple of the heavy Buddha) has an equal claim to fame. Inside the intricately carved ordination chapel, there is a 16th century bronze sculpture weighing a mighty three tons.

It is during the full moon of the 11th month - normally at the end of November - that the most important festival in the Lao Buddhist calendar takes places. To celebrate the annual festival of That Luang, tens of thousands of villagers, many of them dressed in ceremonial silk, or 'pha sin', descend on the city as part of their spiritual pilgrimage to the country's holiest monument. For five days and nights, the grounds of That Luang are the scene of immense candle-lit processions, parades and merit-making ceremonies as the people pay their respects to the Buddha and make offerings of garlanded flowers, incense sticks and food to the monks who are gathered there. The ceremonies culminate with the Buddhist faithful lining up inside the temple courtyard to donate money to the upkeep of the temple and to provide gifts for the monks to take back to their village wats.

Street Carnival

Outside the grounds of That Luang, the atmosphere resembles a giant street carnival. At night, crowds of people flock to listen to live bands performing on specially-erected stages, a stone's throw from where the religious festivities take place. Stalls overflow onto the nearby sidewalks piled high with barbecued chicken, noodle soup and an abundance of beer and local whisky.

Whilst the week-long That Luang fair provides one way for the Lao Loum to make merit, other temples also offer the opportunity for salvation. In nearby Wat Si Muang, believers arrive daily with offerings of bananas, coconuts and boiled eggs for the resident guardian spirits. The temple is believed to have been constructed over a pit where a pregnant woman was ritually sacrificed. These days it is recognized throughout the city as the place where the faithful may be granted their wishes.

The Heartlands

It is in springtime that the rice fields that surround Vientiane and the Nam Ngum Reservoir to the north take on their finest hue. As the heavy rains of the previous months give way to calming sunshine, the paddies turn from green to yellow and finally to a golden brown, signalling the start of the harvesting season. For the Lao Loum, rice is the single most important crop in the country, grown by some 80% of the population and consumed by villagers even in the furthest flung regions. Preparation of the seed beds and ploughing are almost always the responsibility of the men. The women, for their part, transplant and weed the paddies as well as pounding the rice.

Harvesting generally begins at the end of October or early November when adult members of the village put aside their ordinary tasks to labour in the fields. Like an army of ants on the move, they sweep through the rich heartlands with their scythes glinting, leaving giant mounds of rice in their wake. Only when the crop has been stored away in barns do the Lao Loum relax in the knowledge that they have food for their families in the months to come.

But the lives of these rural people are also changing. Where once ox carts were the norm, now mini-tractors often carry the workers to the fields. New roads and bridges are also opening up formerly isolated districts of the country, bringing development that as little as a decade ago would have been almost unthinkable. In the cities, the signs of progress are especially striking, with ugly concrete buildings and shophouses fast replacing traditional wooden houses that have been used for generations. But whilst the low-land people may increasingly dream of a motorbike or a television, the lives of the majority of these people continue to be tied to the soil, to the local temple and to their close knit village communities.

Giant Caves

East of Vientiane, the Chinese shop houses and bustling urban markets give way to plains and further afield to the splendour of limestone cliffs rising up into the distance. The lush mountain landscape forms part of Khammuan Province, a region rarely visited by tourists, despite its immense beauty and its relative proximity to the towns of Savannakhet and Vientiane.

Journeying through this spectacular countryside of stone forests and pristine turquoise streams, we enter caves that extend up to 8 kilometres into the hillside. Inside the mouth of Tham Konglor, rocks sculpted like buffalo heads and elephant trunks emerge from the darkness, their shapes momentarily lit up by the flickering of an oil lamp. The only sounds come from the rushing of water over invisible rapids as well as the sudden roar of an outboard motor as a dugout canoe sails through this vast inner cavern before emerging from the cave further up-river.

Beyond the tin mines of Bor Phon Thieu, carved out of the reddish brown hillside, the route continues south alongside the banks of the Mekong. Passing the dusty towns of Tha Kaek and Sebongfai, we enter the historic city of Savannakhet, home to some of the finest remaining Franco-Chinese architecture in the region. Although Savannakhet has long since outgrown its historical roots, colonial era houses still line parts of Khanthabouli and Phetslath roads, their imposing facades and flaking wooden shutters providing a delightful glimpse of life on the river in the early days of the 20th century.

Preceding pages: Lao Loum settlement in remote Sanamxai District, Attapeu Province.
Left page: Monks repaint their temple in the sunshine, Vientiane.
Above, top: Prize fighting cock, Savannakhet Province. – bottom: A parade through the streets of Vientiane.

Sunset over the Mekong River, Ban Nakasang, Champassak Province.

Herders in search of new pastures, Sekong Province, Southern Laos.

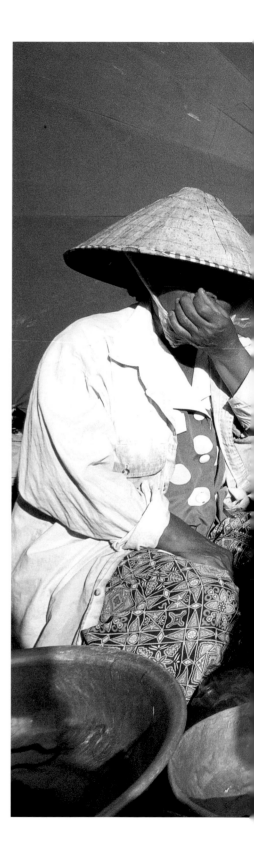

Top: Harvesting the rice, Van Vieng, Vientiane Prefecture.
Bottom: Ploughing the rice paddies, Southern Laos.

Talat Thong Khan Kham fruit and vegetable market, Vientiane.

Passenger boats on the banks of the Mekong, Pakse, Champassak Province.

Top: French colonial architecture, Pakse.
Bottom: Bridge over the Se Bang Fai River, Savannakhet Province.

Preceding pages– Left: Village elder up in the hills of Central Laos. Right: Separating the rice husks from the chaff, Sayaboury Province.
Above: Buddhist faithful make offerings at That Luang, Laos' most revered temple.

Top: Annual Buddhist parade, That Luang, Vientiane.
Bottom: Candle-lit procession, That Luang, Vientiane.

Child at play inside Wat Hai Sok compound, Vientiane.

Locals celebrate a Buddhist holiday, Wat Mixayaram, in Vientiane.

Colourful processions mark the climax of the That Luang festival, Vientiane.

Ritual offerings to the Buddha and the spirits, Wat Ong Teu, Vientiane.

The venerated golden stupa of That Luang, Vientiane.

Top: Patuxai monument known as the Gate of Triumph, Vientiane.
Bottom: Wat Chom Thong, Don Kong Island.
Following pages: Buddhist thanks-giving ceremony, That Luang.

THE FAR PROVINCES

The plane banked over the Plain of Jars and turned steeply to the left. Below the twin propeller aircraft lay pot-holed rice fields tapering off into the distant foothills. A few water buffalo grazed contentedly in the midday-heat. Nothing else disturbed this tranquil scene. This air of rustic splendour, however, belies the stark reality. For these craters, the size of houses, are the result not of the recent monsoon rains but of the secret bombing campaign carried out by the US airforce during the Vietnam war in a bid to defeat the communist inspired Pathet Lao army.

According to the latest documentary evidence, between 1964 and 1973, when the bombing campaign finally came to an end, the US airforce flew some 580,000 raids over neutral Laos, equivalent to one sortie every eight minutes for nine consecutive years. In all, they dropped more than two million metric tons of bombs, equivalent to ten tons per square kilometer, or approximately half a ton of explosives for every inhabitant. That gives Laos the dubious distinction of being probably the most bombed country on earth.

Neither the often quoted statistics nor the sight of these giant craters, however, can convey the extent of the devastation inflicted upon these simple farming people by the use of bombs, mines and other explosive devices. Some of the highest casualties were caused by the use of baby bombs, the size of tennis balls with a killing range of 150 metres. Fragmentation devices, allegedly used for the first time in Laos by the US military for experimental purposes, also caused other horrific injuries. Even the rules of engagement normally applied to war zones were never imposed on Laos. Whereas in neighbouring Cambodia and Vietnam US pilots were prohibited from dropping bombs within 1km of a temple, in Laos no such restrictions existed.

More than 25 years after the conflict ended, the local people are still counting the cost of this clandestine war. On the vast tablelands of this central province, where rice farming and slash and burn agriculture continue to be the primary source of employment, unexploded ordnance continues to kill and maim children and other innocent civilians, despite large scale de-mining by western nations who are attempting to erase this chapter of western imperialism. Here, in this remote and beautiful landscape, they provide an ever-present reminder of this tragic war.

Plain of Jars

Dawn over the Plain of Jars is almost akin to a mystical experience. In the half-darkness, these looming primordial urns lie silhouetted against the horizon, reminders of a bygone age that even now archaeologists are still grappling to understand. In total, some 275 jars lie scattered on this site at Thong Hai Hin, each jar made from a single piece of sandstone or granite and weighing up to six tons apiece. Some of the jars have lids. Others are in fragments, blasted by the bombs that were dropped on the area by the US pilots. Archaeologists now claim that the jars could date as far back as 2,000 years and provide vital clues to Laos' early civilization.

But who were these people who left behind these stone urns measuring as much as one metre wide and two metres high? Even more intriguing, how did the local people transport these imposing monoliths from the distant stone quarries on the borders of Xieng Khuang Province to this far flung district?

As yet, only minimal research has been carried out on the origins of the jars due to lack of financial resources and the sheer complexities involved in working in this remote part of the country. Studies undertaken by French and Japanese archaeological teams do, however, point to one widely accepted conclusion: that the jars are funerary urns dating back to the Iron Age. Similar funerary urns have also been found in remote parts of Southern China as well as Central Vietnam.

On the outside of one jar, a team of archaeologists discovered the relief of a human figure. Large quantities of beads, bells and bracelets as well as iron knives, arrowheads and spears have also been unearthed in other related sites dating back to between 300 BC and AD300. One theory is that the bodies were first cremated in the nearby limestone caves. The ashes were then placed in these gargantuan urns together with jewellery and other possessions destined to be taken to the next world.

The Lao people have come up with a more fanciful solution to explain this great enigma. They believe the jars date back to the 6th century when King Khoon Chuong and his troops won a great victory over a cruel chieftain named Chao Angka. To celebrate their victory, the soldiers made bountiful quantities of rice wine, which they fermented in these jars. Legend tells that such was the strength of the Lao people in those days, each man was able to carry a couple of the jars down from the mountainside some seventy kilometers away.

Tragic Secrets

From the town of Phonsavan, rebuilt out of the chaos of war, the road leads east into the heart of this broad and melancholic countryside. In the dusty patchwork of fields, the local farmers winnow the rice or cast finely sewn nets into the remaining pools of water in the hope of catching the small fish known as pla chom to feed their families. Like the jars themselves, however, this landscape screams out its own tragic secrets. In the Hmong Village of Ban Tha Joh, and a short distance further in Ban Na Sala, rusty bomb casings and other debris of war are used as foundations for the people's bamboo and corrugated houses.

Outside these primitive huts, the sight is even more incongruous. In one corner of the muddy yard, rows of flourishing spring onions have been neatly planted in torpedo-shaped bomb casings. Nearby, a litter of pigs feeds out of troughs made from the remains of cluster bombs. Villagers even claim that the aluminium spoons used in the local market are made from the remains of downed American aircraft.

In the remote and mountainous northern Province of Hua Phan, the echoes of war are no less staggering. During the early 1960s, the Pathet Lao converted many of the limestone caves of Vieng Xai into a revolutionary headquarters. From these underground caverns, equipped with telephones, as well as hospitals, ammunition dumps and meeting rooms, senior Pathet Lao leaders, including Prince Souphanouvong and Kaysone Phomvihan, directed insurgency operations, safe from the powerful bombs dropped by B-52s. On several occasions, US planes attacked the caves with napalm and phosphorous rockets, blasting the surrounding areas. But the caves, some of which lead 200 metres into the limestone cliff, remained intact and can be visited to this day.

Village Life

At dusk in the Phou Noi village an old man is cooking. First he catches a chicken from the yard down below; then he knocks the scrawny animal on the head with a metal utensil, plucks the feathers, guts it and throws it into a pot of boiling water placed on the hearth in the centre of the wooden hut. Adding garlic, lemon grass and crushed chillies, he stirs the liquid with a slow circular movement. Smoke from the hearth filters out through the chimney of this wooden hut split into a living room and sleeping quarters.

A short distance from the village, a handful of locals soap themselves down in the muddy stream, wrapped in sarongs to preserve their modesty. A few children play together, kicking a woven rattan ball known as a kataw, which they attempt to keep airborne using their feet. Throughout the towns and villages of the Far Provinces, nightfall brings similar rituals as families come together after their day's labour to share in the meagre fare of sticky rice and vegetables or, for special occasions, a chicken or even wild deer. Typically, they eat around low tables lit by an oil lamp. A separate table is used by the men, whilst another is used by the women and children. When dinner is over, the men stay on to drink rice wine, leaving the women to take care of the children. By 9.30, the village is blanketed in darkness, the only sounds coming from the snorting of pigs below and the screeching of rats as they scurry around in the bamboo rafters.

Elephant Country

High up the mountainside in remote Sayaboury Province, the shrill trumpeting of an elephant echoes through the lush forest canopy. It is still dark and the only light comes from a flickering oil lamp carried by the mahout. Manoeuvering its body down the slippery trail, the elephant, piled high with sacks of maze and rice, descends into the valley, finally reaching the village of Ban By My shortly before dawn. From here the rice is taken and sold in the market at the nearby town of Muang Ngoen.

In the hills of Northwest Laos and along the border with Thailand, hundreds of mahouts work in temporary elephant camps, earning a living from transporting timber and other vital supplies to the villages below. For a heavy log that takes an entire day to drag down the mountainside, the mahouts may be paid as much as US$8. More often than not, they make the trip up and down the mountain pass at least two or three times a day - simply to make ends meet. Camping away from home for up to a week at a time, the mahouts sleep in makeshift huts or under the stars, communicating with each other by banging together bamboo stems that echo through the valleys at night.

In Northern Sayaboury Province alone there are more than 100 elephants and mahouts, constantly moving from one camp to another in search of work. In other parts of this mountainous province, elephants are still relied upon, especially during the monsoon season when flooding makes the narrow roads impassable.

Laos' long association with elephants is firmly entrenched in history. For more than 400 years, the country was known as Land of a Million Elephants. On several occasions, the Lao even went to war over the possession of the revered White Elephant. These days, fewer than 1,500 Asiatic elephants are believed to live in the wild. The number of working elephants also continues to diminish.

Khamu People

A short distance from the village of Nam Noen, the rugged hills of the Annamite Mountains give way temporarily to the scenic low-lying valleys and rice fields of Hua Phan Province, criss-crossed by sudden gorges and by the meandering Nam Noen River. Soon, the simple houses belonging to the Striped and Blue Hmong are replaced by bamboo huts with dirt floors and roofs made from crossed-roof beams. The composition of these villages, along with their proximity to upland rivers and streams, is evidence that we are now entering Khamu territory.

Originally from China's Yunnan Province, the Khamu are the descendants of the oldest Mon-Khmer inhabitants in the country. Belonging to the category known as Lao Theung or Upland Lao, these semi-nomadic people account for as much as 30% of the population. Typically they are slash and burn farmers who grow mountain rice, coffee, tobacco and cotton. They also raise animals and barter their goods for salt and other necessities. As animists, the Khamu believe that the human body contains between 30 and 300 spirits that must be appeased in order to avoid misfortune. Nowadays, although some of the people have converted to Buddhism, the vast majority continues to embrace a traditional way of life that is only gradually being reshaped by the arrival of the modern world.

Opening page: Local bus transport through the remote province of Attapeu in Southern Laos.

Left: A bomb shell in the village of Ban Tha Joh, Xieng Khuang Province. Between 1964 and 1973, the US secretly dropped more bombs on Laos than on any other country on earth.

Preceding pages– Left: The famous Plain of Jars, Xieng Khuang Province. Right: Dawn in Vieng Xai, one of the most remote districts of Hua Phan Province.
Above: Slaughtering a waterbuffalo for market day, Sam Neua.

Top: Minorities from the mountain villages sell their vegetables, Sayaboury Province.
Bottom: Rice planting, Ban Inthi, Attapeu Province.

Waiting for the local bus, Sam Neua, Hua Phan Province.

Village school and clinic, Sam Neua, Hua Phan Province.

Limestone karsts on the Hin Boune River, Khammuan Province.

The subterranean cave of Tham Konglor, Khammuan Province.

Tin mining in the mountain streams of Bor Phun Thieu, Khammuan Province.

Top and bottom: Bor Phun Thieu, Khammuan Province.

Selling baskets in the morning market, Attapeu Province.

Top: Crossing the Sekaman River, Sekong Province.
Bottom: Bolovens Plateau, Tadlo District, Champassak.

CHAMPASSAK AND THE SOUTH

Beyond the town of Pakse, the Mekong River arches to the south, passing under the newly constructed Lao Japanese Bridge before cutting through the pastel coloured mountains of ancient Champassak Province. In the early morning we set sail, passing clusters of fishing boats that dart out from the shoreline only to disappear from view in the mist. A few children wave from the ragged villages built along the banks of the river until finally they are little more than dots on the distant landscape.

According to early chronicles, this historic region, which lies at the southern tip of the country, probably formed part of the Mon Kingdom of Funan, a powerful Indianized Empire that is believed to have flourished from the 1st-6th centuries. For the next 500 years, it fell under the sway of the Khmers, who controlled the great kingdom of Angkor to the southwest. Almost a thousand years later, vestiges of that early civilization can still be seen scattered along the banks of the Mekong – a mass of tumbled down arches and broken lintels cloaked in moss and jungle vegetation.

Passing the ruined 9th century Khmer temple of Oum Muang, the river divides into a maze of fast flowing channels that cut through the countryside. The Lao call this southern stretch of the river See Pan Don, or Four Thousand Islands, after the countless mud banks that emerge out of the Mekong during the dry season. For several months each year, the local people cultivate tomatoes, spring onions and other vegetables on these temporary farmlands. But from June to September, the monsoon rains pour down into the river, submerging the alluvial islands and flooding the surrounding plains.

On the banks of this mighty river, superstitions thrive. Some village elders claim that the river is a naga, or mythical serpent, and that every year before the monsoons arrive, the river must take a human sacrifice. If nobody drowns, the villagers believe the rains will not come and that the crops will die. One local myth even says that the Irrawaddy dolphins, which inhabit the waters off the tip of Don Khon Island, are the reincarnated spirits of fishermen who lost their lives whilst attempting to cross these deadly rapids.

A short distance from the Khone Falls, the river reaches a crescendo, cascading down through narrow rocky channels until further progress by boat becomes impossible. Only on the far side of the rapids does the Mekong take on a different guise, broadening out once again before meandering through Cambodia and finally emptying out into the South China Sea through the sprawling Vietnam Delta.

French Explorers

It was the French officer Francis Garnier who became one of the first men to explore the Mekong. In June 1866, he sailed out of the Cochin Chinese port of Saigon on a naval expedition to navigate the full length of the river. But Garnier's dreams of discovering a new trade route to China were shattered by a succession of natural barriers, including the Khone Falls. "There, in the midst of rocks and grassy islets, an enormous sheet of water leaps headlong from a height of 70 ft, to fall back in floods of foam," wrote the Frenchman on encountering the first of the giant cataracts.

After dismantling the boats and carrying them overland, Garnier and his French crew resumed their expedition. Several months later, the intrepid officer contracted a deadly strain of malaria. He survived the attack of fever and reached Southern China, but was eventually forced to abandon his expedition after clashes with Burmese warlords and hostile hilltribes, returning to Shanghai down the Yangtze Kiang in 1868. Later attempts to navigate the full length of the Mekong also failed, this time as a result of a succession of rapids. According to a 19th century bulletin issued by the Paris Geographical Society, it was virtually impossible to go further north than Vientiane, especially at the time of the monsoon rains when once calm stretches of the river became seething cascades of water. Even during the summer months, sailing on the Mekong was fraught with risks. "On April 1 (1896) we started for the South, this time in double boats lashed together with strong crosspieces," wrote one British national working for the government of Siam. "On the 4th my boat was swamped."

If the French failed to commercially exploit the river, they did successfully solve the problem of transporting goods along it. At the beginning of the 20th century, they built a small railway to bypass the Khone Falls. What is left of the narrow gauge track can still be seen on Don Khone, a twisted heap of metal and a rusting locomotive that mock France's once glorious colonial dreams.

Khmer Ruins

The greatest known Hindu Khmer ruins in Laos lies a short distance inland from the Mekong at the foot of the sacred Phu Khao Mountain. Historians claim that the temple of Wat Phu was built on this hilltop shaped like a lingam, or Shiva phallus, as early as the 6th century – several hundred years before work began on similar pre-Khmer style temples. It was subsequently converted from Hinduism to Buddhism sometime around the 12th century and maintained by the kings of Angkor until well into the 14th century.

Although Wat Phu cannot compare in scale with the celebrated Angkor Wat in neighbouring Cambodia, its ruined sandstone pavilions and its carvings of Shiva the Hindu deity and Indra riding on a three-headed elephant are believed to be the oldest of their kind in the whole of Southeast Asia. The extraordinary composition of the temple complex, together with the mythological reliefs on the sides of the stone entrances, also reflects the rich symbolism of the Hindu cosmos. From the base of the monument, a grand processional avenue flanked by stone pillars ascends through three levels from the realm of man to the mountain peak representing Mount Meru - the traditional seat of the gods.

The most impressive time to visit this hillside sanctuary is during the monsoon season when the faded sculptures are silhouetted against dark storm clouds and when the monument takes on an air of solitary grandeur. The annual spring festival of Wat Phu - held at the time of the full moon in February - also attracts tens of thousands of local people and Buddhist pilgrims who descend on the temple from all over the region to take part in processions, merit-making ceremonies and other religious activities.

Far from being the only archaeological site in Champassak Province, Wat Phu is just one component in a rich archaeological landscape. Other Khmer ruins can be found on both banks of the Mekong and up in the mountains to the west. According to the latest research carried out by UNESCO, a road may even have extended from the Nandi Hall at Wat Phu all the way to Angkor, situated over 200 km away.

Coffee Route

East of Pakse, the road climbs through increasingly picturesque countryside towards the distant plateau. Soon the cattle-grazing pastures and banana plantations of the plains give way to rows of coffee trees. The French settlers originally introduced these vast arabica coffee plantations back in the 1920s and 1930s. As a result, the Bolovens Plateau became known as the Coffee Route.

Nowadays coffee continues to bring prosperity to the region. Such is the reputation of the arabica and robusta produced on the Bolovens Plateau, that every year they are exported to some of the furthest flung countries in the world. Tea, cardamom and tropical fruits, including the potent smelling durian, are also fast transforming this fertile southern region into one of the most productive in the country.

Beyond Tha Teng, the road plunges back into the wilderness, running alongside the plateau, before rejoining the main route near the popular village of Tadlo. Of the 68 ethnic minorities found in Laos, some 12 of them are found in this pristine area, liberally sprinkled with waterfalls and streams. One of the most fascinating tribes in this region is the Alak, an Austro-Indonesian ethno-linguistic group renowned for the face tattoos of their women as well as their circular palm and thatched villages. Other minorities like the Khatu, a Mon Khmer people, are better known for their water buffalo sacrifices, which they hold annually to appease the spirits of their great ancestors.

Village Ceremonies

Our arrival in the village of Tanhukseua is welcomed by euphoric shouts. To the sound of loud pop music blaring out from a decrepit pair of speakers, the people of this Nha Heune settlement lead us to a shady spot under a large tarpaulin. In the centre of the ground, surrounded by wedding guests and village elders, is a giant clay jar out of which emerges several dozen bamboo straws. First my guide takes a long sip of this fiercely potent rice wine, then it is my turn to drink the fire water as the entire village watches transfixed.

For three days and three nights, the Nha Heune will take it in turns to drink the Lao Lao in the belief that this will bring good health, prosperity and happiness to the newly married couple. The minority people consider it the height of bad manners to turn down a drink until each gallon container of rice wine has been drained to the very bottom.

If the Nha Heune enjoy a good party, so do plenty of the other minorities in Southern Laos. In Ta-Oy villages throughout the region, the people hold water buffalo sacrifices to celebrate the New Year. As soon as the animals have been bludgeoned to death using machetes, the buffalo meat is offered first to the spirits and then to the village inhabitants, who believe that it will bring them strength and good fortune. Other minorities have adopted different superstitions. The Alak believe that to test the prospects of marriage between members of the same tribe, they must kill a chicken and inspect its entrails to see whether these indicate an auspicious union.

Border Lands

Crossing the Annamite Mountain Range, the dirt road from Sekong to Attapeu twists and turns through the hillside, affording glimpses of the forested plateau shrouded in low-lying cloud. In places the road is in appalling condition. In others, it is being widened as part of a government plan to open up the most far-flung regions of the country. After little more than an hour, our vehicle draws to a halt on the banks of the Sekaman River. Loaded onto a rusty pontoon, it is then towed to the far side by a motor-powered canoe.

On the far bank, the dirt track continues through sparse forest with occasional views of the distant plateau. Rarely is there any sign of life except for a scattering of thatched huts and the sight of villagers stalking the flatlands for game, clutching finely-carved single-barrel shot guns. It's another fine drive to the town of Attapeu, perched on the confluence of the Kong and Sekhaman Rivers. Known to the Lao as 'Garden Town' after its many flowered lanes and lush tropical plants, this picturesque town borders one of the most beautiful, but inaccessible regions of Laos, home to a scattering of Ta-oy, Lavene and Alak villages.

From Attapeu, we travel east, following a labyrinth of unsign-posted dirt tracks that lead towards the Vietnamese border. Eventually, however, we can go no further, brought to a halt by appalling roads, by fears of unexploded ordnance and by the floods that even in October make much of this area impassable. And so we take the route back to Attapeu and beyond to the town of Paksong, before ending our journey in Pakse on the banks of the great Mekong River.

Opening page: The annual Wat Phu festival held in ancient Champassak Province, Southern Laos.

Left: A passenger boat speeds through Si Phan Don, known as the Four Thousand Islands region in Champassak Province.

Preceding pages – Left: Somphamit Falls, Don Khon Island. – Right: Local fisherman with his catch, Somphamit Falls.
Above: The turbulent waters of the River Mekong, Southern Laos.

122

Top: The dramatic Khong Papheng Falls, Champassak Province.
Bottom: Dusk on the banks of the Mekong, Ban Khinak.

Left: The ancient Hindu Khmer ruins of Wat Phu, Champassak Province.
Right: The annual three-day Wat Phu Festival.

Offerings to the Buddha and to the mountain gods, Wat Phu Festival.

Top: Giving alms to the monks, Wat Phu.
Bottom: Early morning rush hour, Southern Laos.

Local bus transport in remote Attapeu Province, Southern Laos.

Na Heune wedding celebrations, Ban Thanhukseua, Bolovens Plateau.

Banana harvest, Ban Houay Hun, Bolovens Plateau.

Coffee plantation worker, Tha Teng District, Bolovens Plateau.
Final page: Monk at work, Savannakhet Province.